JUN   2006

THE DIGESTIVE SYSTEM

EARLY BIRD
BODY SYSTEMS

BY REBECCA L. JOHNSON

LERNER PUBLICATIONS COMPANY • MINNEAPOLIS

Lerner Publications Company
A division of Lerner Publishing Group
241 First Avenue North
Minneapolis, MN 55401 U.S.A.

Website address: www.lernerbooks.com

Library of Congress Cataloging-in-Publication Data

Johnson, Rebecca L.
    The digestive system / by Rebecca L. Johnson.
      p.   cm. — (Early bird body systems)
    Includes index.
    ISBN: 0–8225–1247–5 (lib. bdg. : alk. paper)
    1. Digestive organs—Juvenile literature. I. Title. II. Series.
QP145.J64 2005
611'.3—dc22   2004002380

Manufactured in the United States of America
1 2 3 4 5 6 – JR – 10 09 08 07 06 05

CONTENTS

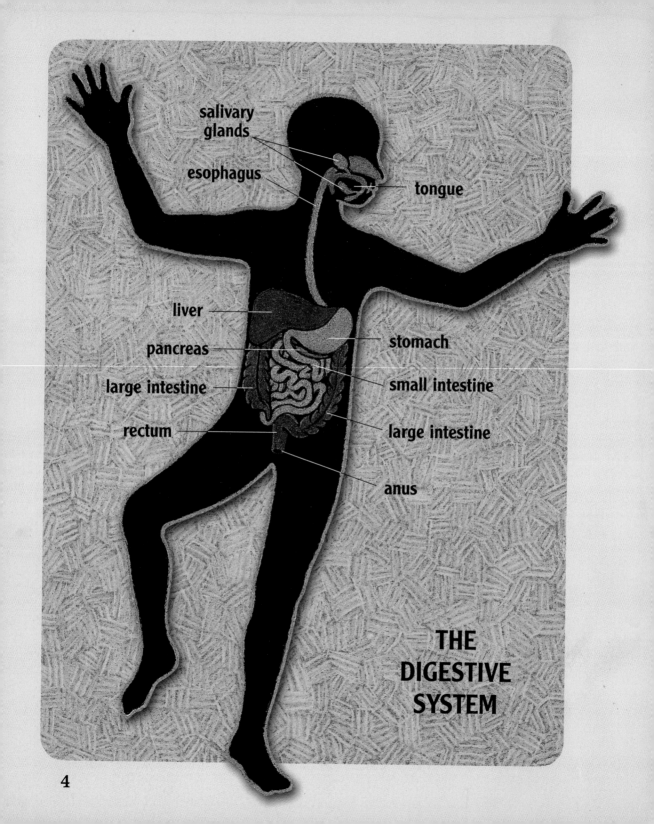

salivary
glands

esophagus

tongue

liver

pancreas

stomach

large intestine

small intestine

rectum

large intestine

anus

**THE
DIGESTIVE
SYSTEM**

BE A WORD DETECTIVE

Can you find these words as you read about the digestive system? Be a detective and try to figure out what they mean. You can turn to the glossary on page 46 for help.

acid	liver	rectum
digest	mucus	saliva
digestive juice	nutrients	trachea
epiglottis	organs	villi
esophagus	pancreas	

CHAPTER 1

FUEL FOR LIFE

When you're hungry, pizza tastes great! What does your stomach do when you're hungry?

Mmmm! There's fresh, hot pizza! You are so hungry. Your stomach is growling. You take a big bite. Cheese, crust, and sauce mix together in your mouth.

Is pizza your favorite food? Maybe it's pudding, peaches, or pot roast. There are thousands of foods. Think of all the kinds of food you eat.

Food is fuel for your body. Eating many kinds of food keeps your body working well.

Food is more than yummy tastes or crunchy mouthfuls. Food is fuel. It gives your body and your mind energy. Good food keeps you healthy and strong.

Eating good food keeps you strong and active.

Eating good food also helps you think.

But food must be changed before your body can use it. Your body must digest (dye-JEHST) it first.

When you digest food, it is broken down into nutrients (NOO-tree-ehnts). Nutrients feed your body and keep it working well.

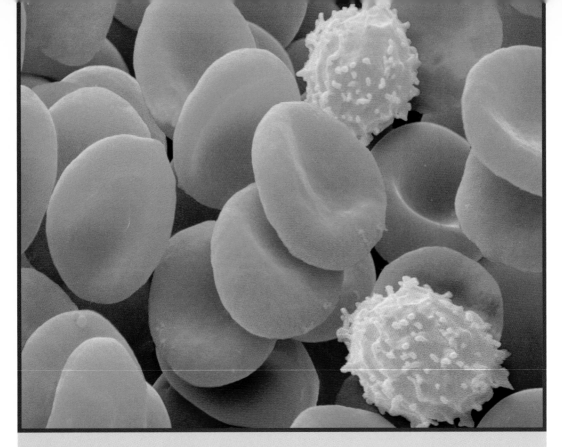

Blood is made up of cells. So are muscles, skin, bones, and other body parts.

Your body is made up of billions of cells. Cells are like tiny building blocks. They work together to form every part of you. Your skin, bones, and muscles are made of cells. Cells make up your eyes, heart, and all of your other organs too.

Your body uses nutrients to fix damaged cells. It uses nutrients to make new cells. It uses nutrients for energy too. That energy gives you the power to live and grow.

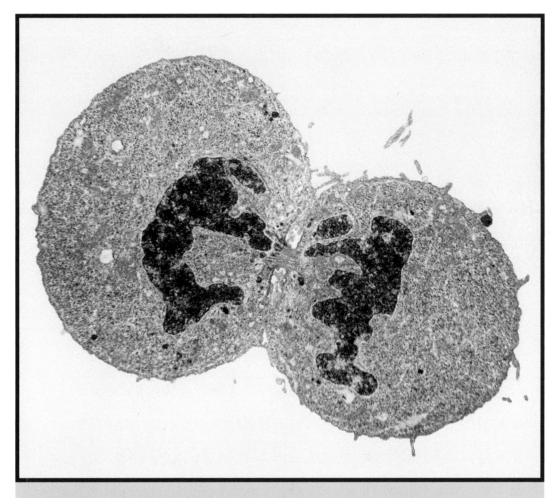

Nutrients give cells what they need to grow, divide, and work. This cell is about to split into two cells.

CHAPTER 2

IN YOUR MOUTH

You start to take a bite of your pizza. Where will it go?

Food is digested in your digestive system. A system is a way of doing things. Your digestive system is like a long tube. It has a few bulges here and there. The tube twists and turns all the way through your body.

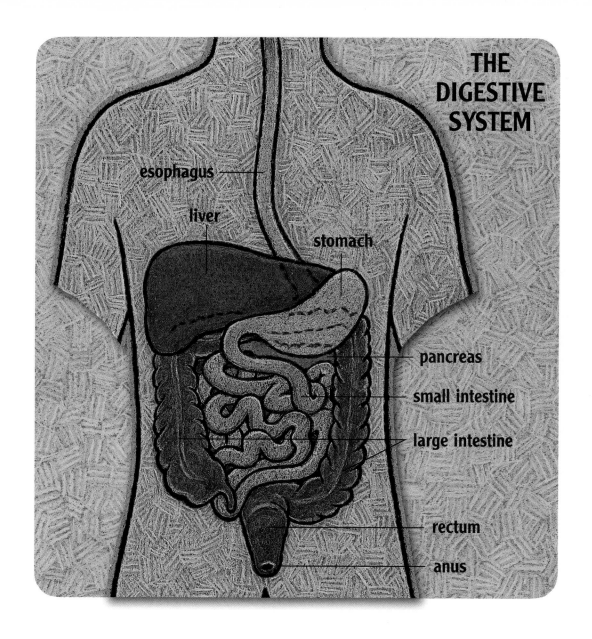

THE
DIGESTIVE
SYSTEM

esophagus

liver

stomach

pancreas

small intestine

large intestine

rectum

anus

Remember that bite of pizza? It is about to enter your digestive system. It has a long trip ahead. So let's follow that food!

As you chew, your teeth break up the pizza. You chew it into smaller and smaller pieces.

You have several kinds of teeth in your mouth. They have different shapes. Each kind of tooth works on food in a different way. Your front teeth tear your food. And your back teeth grind your food.

Your front teeth have sharp edges. They are good for biting off a chunk of food.

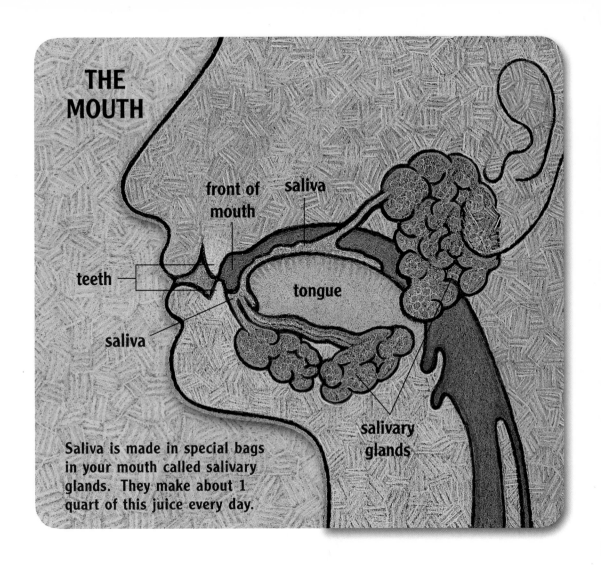

THE MOUTH

front of mouth

saliva

teeth

tongue

saliva

salivary glands

Saliva is made in special bags in your mouth called salivary glands. They make about 1 quart of this juice every day.

As you chew, a liquid mixes with the food in your mouth. This watery liquid is called saliva (suh-LYE-vuh). Saliva is one kind of digestive juice. Digestive juices help break down food in your digestive system.

Chewed food gets soft and slimy as it mixes with saliva. Your tongue shapes the food into a lump. When you are ready to swallow, your tongue pushes the lump. The lump moves to the back of your mouth, where your throat begins.

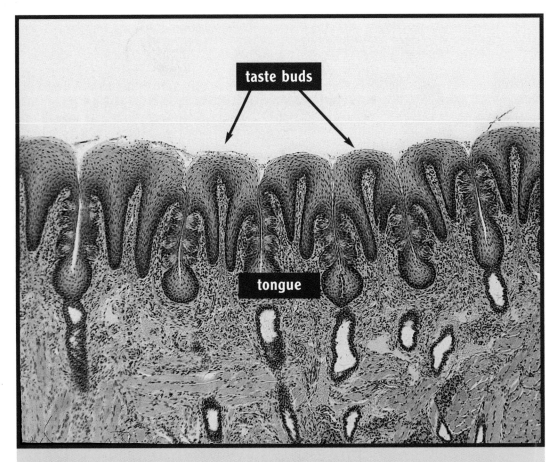

Little bumps on your tongue are called taste buds. They help you taste the flavors in food.

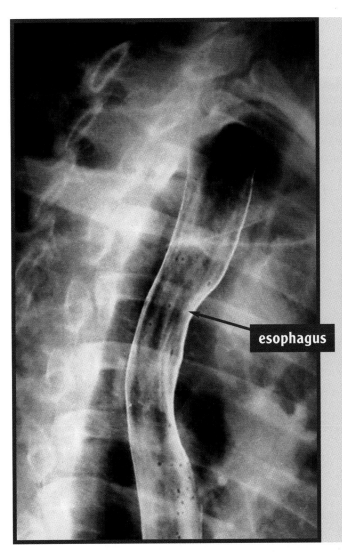

esophagus

Your esophagus is about 10 inches long. It connects your mouth to your stomach. This X-ray photo shows part of the esophagus.

Your throat sits at the top of two tubes. The esophagus (ih-SAH-fuh-guhs) is the tube that leads to your stomach. The other tube is the trachea (TRAY-kee-uh). It leads to your lungs.

At the top of your trachea is a little flap of skin. It is called the epiglottis (eh-pih-GLAH-tihs). When you swallow, the epiglottis flops down. It closes the trachea. That way, food doesn't get into your lungs by mistake.

THE EPIGLOTTIS AT WORK

lump of food

nose

mouth

tongue

epiglottis up

tongue

esophagus

epiglottis down

lump of food

to stomach

to lungs

trachea

The epiglottis guards the trachea. It keeps food from "going down the wrong way" when you swallow.

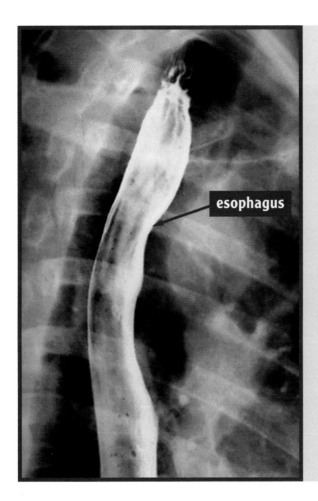

esophagus

Muscles in the wall of the esophagus squeeze together to move food down to the stomach.

Swallowed food doesn't just fall down the esophagus to your stomach. Muscles are in the wall of the esophagus. The muscles squeeze behind the lump of food. The squeezing pushes the food along. It's like squeezing toothpaste out of a tube.

At the bottom of the esophagus is a ring of muscles. The muscles can open and close that end of the esophagus. Most of the time, the ring is tightly closed. But when food comes down the tube, the muscles relax. They let the lump of food move into your stomach.

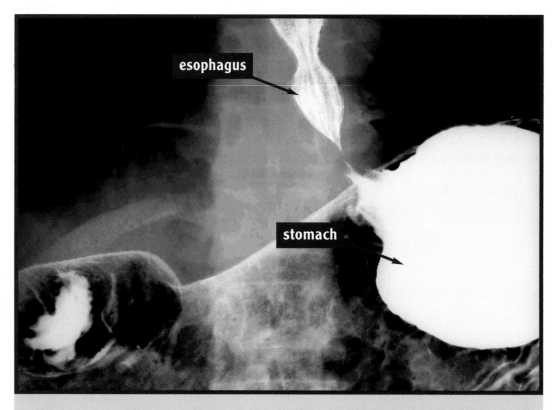

The ring of muscles at the bottom of your esophagus opens only when food is coming down. This keeps food that is already in the stomach from moving back up into the esophagus.

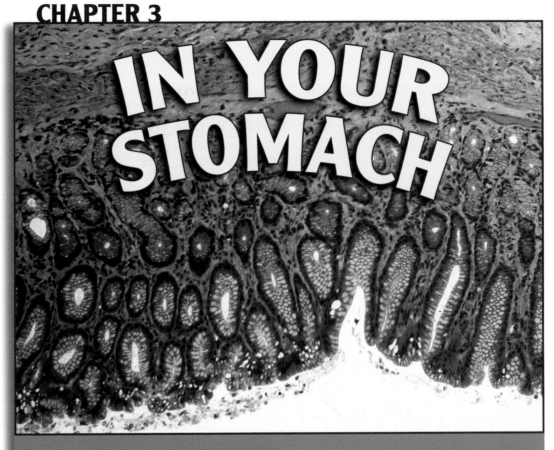

CHAPTER 3

IN YOUR STOMACH

Special cells line the wall of your stomach. What do some of these cells do?

Digestion continues when food reaches your stomach. The stomach has a stretchy wall. The wall is covered with special cells. Some of these cells make digestive juice. The juice continues breaking down the food.

Other stomach cells make acid. Acid is a liquid that softens food. It also kills any germs in the food.

And other cells make slippery, slimy mucus (MYOO-kuhs). Mucus coats the food. Mucus also coats the wall of the stomach.

A coating of mucus protects the wall of your stomach.
Mucus keeps acid from burning your stomach.

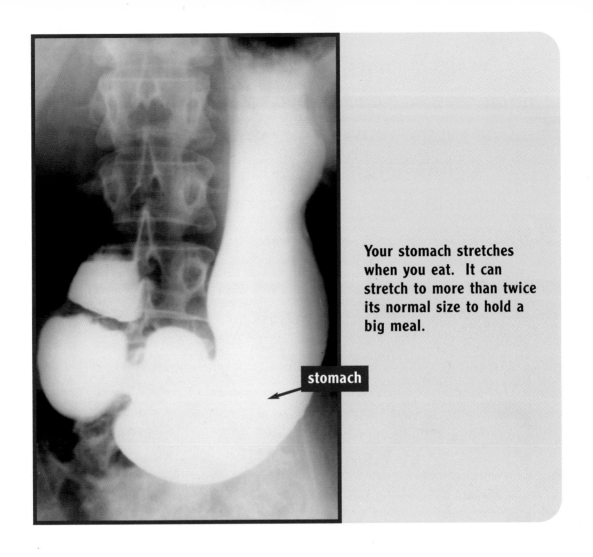

Your stomach stretches when you eat. It can stretch to more than twice its normal size to hold a big meal.

stomach

About every 20 seconds, muscles in the stomach wall squeeze. This squeezing mixes the food with digestive juice, acid, and mucus. This mixing goes on for several hours. It turns the pizza you ate into a soupy liquid.

At the bottom of the stomach is a small hole. The hole is surrounded by a ring of muscles.

Every few minutes, the ring of muscles relaxes. The hole opens. Some of the soupy liquid squirts out of your stomach and into the small intestine.

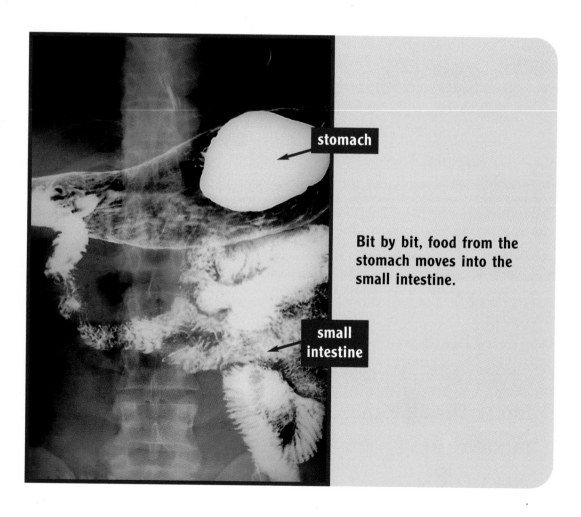

stomach

Bit by bit, food from the stomach moves into the small intestine.

small intestine

CHAPTER 4

TAKING UP NUTRIENTS

If you could stretch your small intestine out straight, it would be about as long as a school bus. Where in your body is your small intestine ?

Your small intestine is a narrow tube that loops around and around in your belly. It is the longest part of your digestive system. It is about 20 feet long.

When food enters the beginning of the small intestine, more digestive juices are added. These juices come from two organs called the pancreas (PAN-kree-uhs) and the liver (LIH-vuhr).

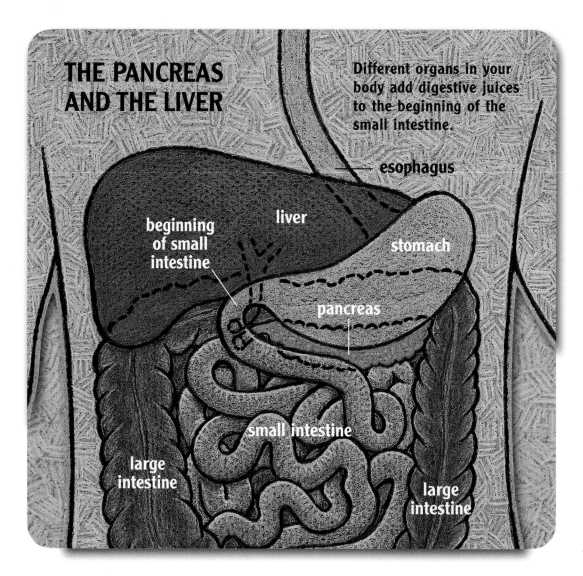

THE PANCREAS AND THE LIVER

Different organs in your body add digestive juices to the beginning of the small intestine.

esophagus

liver

stomach

beginning of small intestine

pancreas

small intestine

large intestine

large intestine

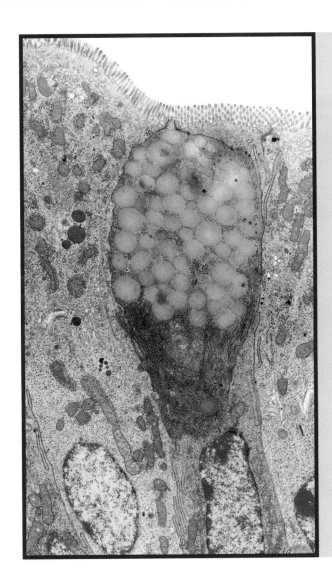

Cells in the wall of the small intestine make mucus. The green and blue cell is a mucus-making cell.

Muscles in the wall of the small intestine squeeze together. They push the food slowly along. More mucus is added to keep the food moving smoothly.

Slowly but surely, the digestive juices finish their work. The pizza becomes a mix of nutrients. The nutrients are very small.

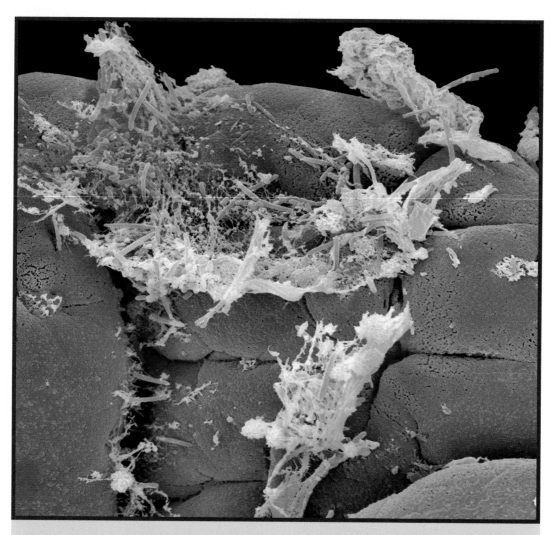

This photo was taken with a microscope. It shows tiny bits of digested food that are stuck to the wall of the small intestine.

Millions and millions of bumps called villi cover the inside surface of the small intestine.

The inside surface of the small intestine is covered with millions of tiny bumps. These bumps are called villi (VIH-lye). They are shaped like tiny fingers. The walls of the villi are very thin.

Inside the villi are tiny blood vessels. Blood vessels are tubes that carry blood through your body. Nutrients can go through the thin walls of the villi and into your blood.

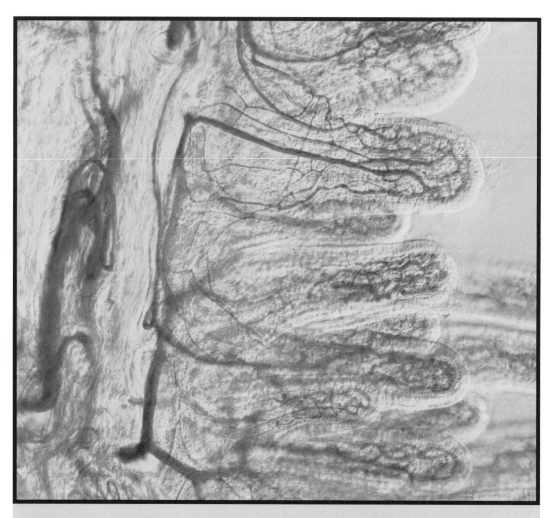

Nutrients move from the small intestine into tiny blood vessels.

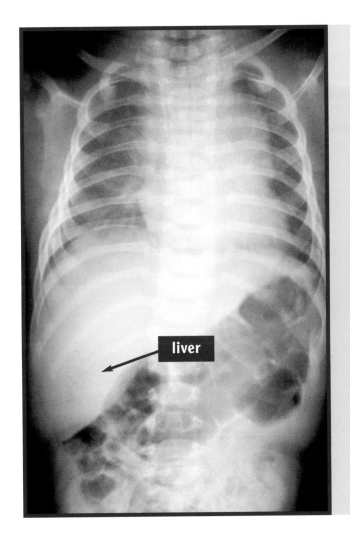

liver

The liver takes up a lot of space in your belly.

Blood carries nutrients to the liver. The liver cleans the blood. It strains out nutrients when they arrive.

Some nutrients are stored in the liver. They stay there until the body needs them.

Other nutrients leave the liver quickly. Before they go, the liver changes them. It makes the nutrients easier for cells to use. Blood carries these nutrients all around your body. They are delivered to each and every one of your cells.

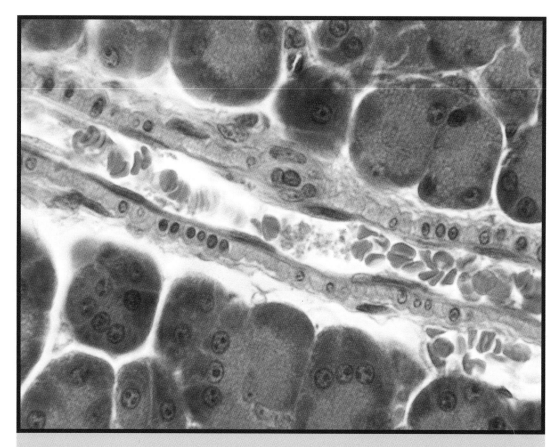

Nutrients are carried in the blood. The blood delivers nutrients to cells.

Nutrients help you grow tall.

Your body uses some nutrients to grow taller. It uses others to build strong bones and teeth. Still other nutrients are used by muscles to help you move.

Nutrients are also needed for repairing your body. When you skin your knee, your cells use nutrients to make a scab. The scab covers the wound. Nutrients also help new cells grow to replace the skin that was lost.

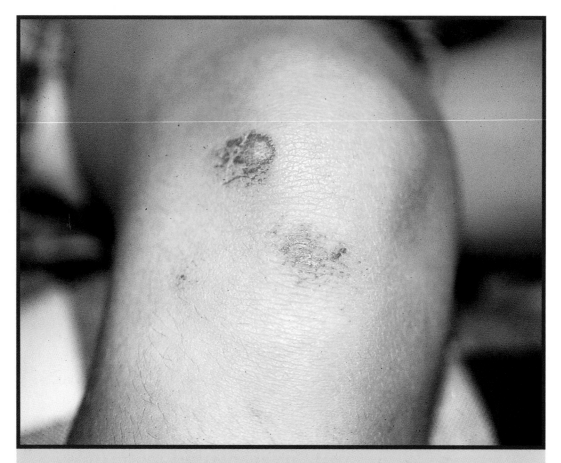

When you scrape your knee, some nutrients are used to fix damaged cells.

CHAPTER 5

GETTING RID OF WASTES

The large intestine begins where the small intestine ends. What is left when food reaches the end of your small intestine?

By the time food reaches the end of your small intestine, digestion is finished. Most of the nutrients in your pizza have passed into your blood. All that is left is waste.

Waste moves into the large intestine. The large intestine is the last part of the digestive system. It is wider than the small intestine. But it is only about 5 feet long. That's about as long as a bicycle.

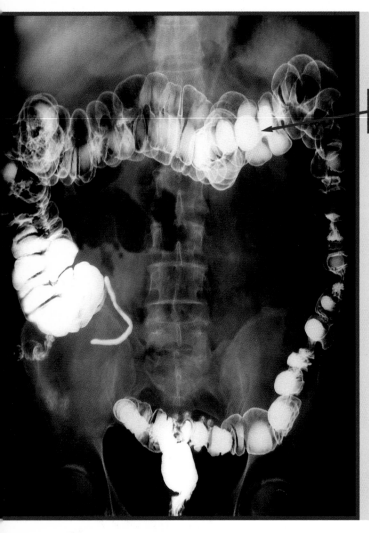

large intestine

Your large intestine runs along the top of your small intestine and curves around your belly.

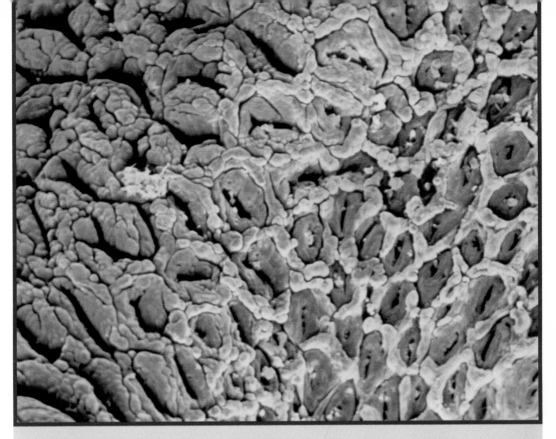

Villi cover the wall of the small intestine *(left)*. Where the large intestine begins *(right)*, there are no villi.

The large intestine forms a big loop in your belly. It runs up your right side. Then it goes across your middle and down your left side. The last part of the large intestine is the rectum.

The walls of the large intestine are smooth on the inside. There are no villi here.

Muscles help push waste through your large intestine. As waste moves along, it loses water. The water goes through the wall of the large intestine. It is used by your cells.

The waste becomes more solid. It is shaped into soft masses called feces (FEE-seez).

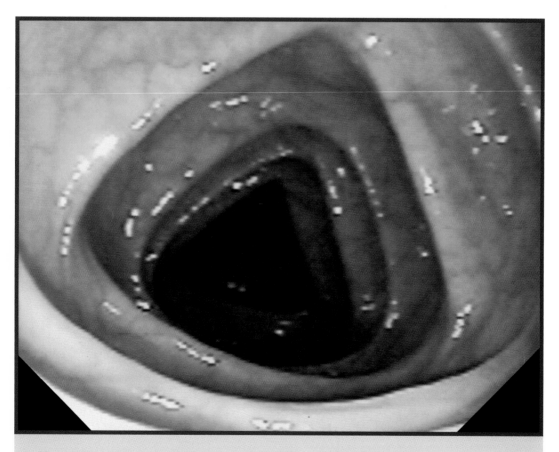

Muscles in the wall of the large intestine push wastes along.

Getting rid of waste is a part of digestion. After you go to the bathroom, it's important to wash your hands.

Eventually, feces get to the rectum. There is an opening at the end of the rectum. It is called the anus (AY-nuhs). Most of the time, the anus is held closed by a ring of muscles. When you have to go to the bathroom, these muscles relax. The feces pass out of your body.

It takes about 24 hours for a meal to move through your digestive system. The exact time depends on the size of your meal. It also depends on the kinds of food you ate.

Once you swallow food, you don't have to think about digestion. You can't control it. It just happens. But you can control what kinds of food you eat. You can control how much you eat.

Eating healthy foods will give your body the nutrients it needs.

DIGESTION TIMES

These pictures show how food moves through your digestive system. The times tell how long it takes for food to get from your mouth to each part of the system.

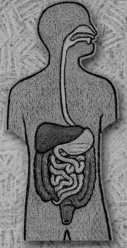

You start to eat.

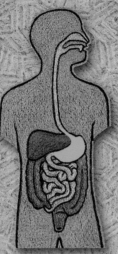

½ hour: your stomach is full.

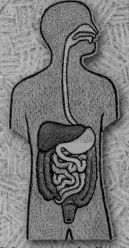

2 hours: partly digested food from the stomach enters the small intestine.

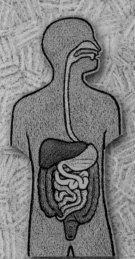

6 hours: your stomach is nearly empty.

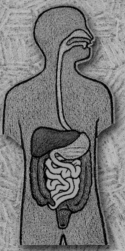

12 hours: nutrients are being absorbed in the small intestine.

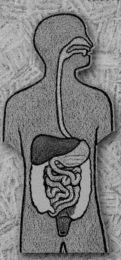

18 hours: wastes are forming in the large intestine.

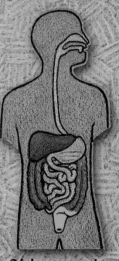

24 hours: wastes are ready to leave the body.

If you eat too much, you take in more nutrients than your body can use. Some extra nutrients are stored in your body as fat. Too much stored fat is unhealthy.

When you're hungry for snacks, healthy foods will give your body what it needs.

Eating good food gives you energy to play sports.

If you eat too little, you may not get all the nutrients you need. If you eat only a few kinds of foods, you won't get all the nutrients you need either. Eating well gives you the energy to do the things you want to do. If you feed your body the right fuel, you'll be healthy and strong.

A NOTE TO ADULTS
ON SHARING A BOOK

When you share a book with a child, you show that reading is important. To get the most out of the experience, read in a comfortable, quiet place. Turn off the television and limit other distractions, such as telephone calls. Be prepared to start slowly. Take turns reading parts of this book. Stop occasionally and discuss what you're reading. Talk about the photographs. If the child begins to lose interest, stop reading. When you pick up the book again, revisit the parts you have already read.

BE A VOCABULARY DETECTIVE

The word list on page 5 contains words that are important in understanding the topic of this book. Be word detectives and search for the words as you read the book together. Talk about what the words mean and how they are used in the sentence. Do any of these words have more than one meaning? You will find the words defined in a glossary on page 46.

WHAT ABOUT QUESTIONS?

Use questions to make sure the child understands the information in this book. Here are some suggestions:

> What did this paragraph tell us? What does this picture show? What do you think we'll learn about next? Why do you need to digest your food? What does the liver do? What can you do to keep your body healthy? What is your favorite part of the book? Why?

If the child has questions, don't hesitate to respond with questions of your own, such as What do *you* think? Why? What is it that you don't know? If the child can't remember certain facts, turn to the index.

INTRODUCING THE INDEX

The index helps readers find information without searching through the whole book. Turn to the index on page 48. Chose an entry such as *mucus* and ask the child to use the index to find out how mucus helps digestion. Repeat with as many entries as you like. Ask the child to point out the differences between an index and a glossary. (The index helps readers find information, while the glossary tells readers what words mean.)

LEARN MORE ABOUT
THE DIGESTIVE SYSTEM

BOOKS

Cromwell, Sharon. *Why Does My Tummy Rumble When I'm Hungry (And Other Questions about the Digestive System).* Des Plaines, IL: Rigby Interactive Library, 1998. This book answers simple questions about how digestion works.

Holub, Joan. *I Have a Weird Brother Who Digested a Fly.* Morton Grove: IL: Albert Whitman & Company, 1999. A silly, rhyming story is supplemented with text that explains the basics of digestion.

Maynard, Jacqui. *I Know Where My Food Goes.* Cambridge, MA: Candlewick Press, 1999. A boy and his mother talk about the digestive system before they eat their lunch.

Showers, Paul. *What Happens to a Hamburger?* New York: HarperCollins, 2001. In this bright, illustrated book, a short-order cook explains digestion, step-by-step.

Swanson, Diane. *Burp! The Most Interesting Book You'll Ever Read about Eating.* Tonawanda, NY: Kids Can Press, 2001. This book is filled with strange and wacky facts about food, nutrition, and the digestive system.

WEBSITES

Pathfinders for Kids: The Digestive System—The Food Factory
http://infozone.imcpl.org/kids_diges.htm
This Web page has a list of resources you can use to learn more about the digestive system.

My Body
http://www.kidshealth.org/kid/body/mybody.html
This fun website has information on the systems of the human body, plus movies, games, and activities.

Fruits and Vegetables at Enchanted Learning
http://www.zoomschool.com/themes/fruit.shtml
This site has fun crafts, plus information on these healthy foods.

GLOSSARY

acid: liquid made in the stomach that softens food and kills germs in food

digest (dye-JEHST): to break food down so the body can use it

digestive juice: liquid that helps break food down into smaller, simpler parts

epiglottis (eh-pih-GLAH-tihs): the flap of skin that keeps food out of the lungs

esophagus (ih-SAH-fuh-guhs): the tube that connects the mouth to the stomach

liver (LIH-vuhr): a part of the body that makes digestive juice. It also helps the body use digested food.

mucus (MYOO-kuhs): a slimy liquid that covers the walls of the stomach and intestines

nutrients (NOO-tree-ehnts): the parts of food that feed the body and keep it working well

organs: parts of the body that do particular jobs. The stomach, liver, and heart are organs.

pancreas (PAN-kree-uhs): a body part that makes digestive juice

rectum: the end of the large intestine

saliva (suh-LYE-vuh): a liquid in your mouth that helps break down food

trachea (TRAY-kee-uh): the tube that connects the mouth to the lungs

villi (VIH-lye): tiny bumps on the walls of the small intestine

INDEX

Pages listed in **bold** type refer to photographs.